FACT FINDERS

Educational adviser: Arthur Razzell

Life in Ponds and Streams

Leslie Jackman

Illustrated by Fred Anderson and Vanessa Luff
Designed by Faulkner/Marks Partnership

Macmillan Education Limited

Life in Ponds and Streams

Pond Life   page 4

Birds of the Pond   page 6

Insects and Amphibians   page 8

Fishes of the Pond   page 10

Animals and Shell Life   page 12

Stream Life   page 14

Birds of the Stream   page 16

Insects and Shell Life   page 18

Fishes of the Stream   page 20

Glossary   page 22

Index   page 23

Pond Life

Most pond creatures live under the water. But the whirligig beetle spins around on the surface of the water.

The water spider makes a web under the water. It takes bubbles of air from the surface and brushes them into its web so that it can breathe.

Reeds

Water lily

Whirligig beetle

Water spider

Web

Caddis fly larva

Great crested newt

Water boatman

Many plants grow in and around a pond. Reeds grow up out of the water.

Water lily leaves float on the surface. Their flowers grow up into the air.

Kingfisher

Common frog

Toad

Smooth newt

Water vole

Water scorpion

Birds of the Pond

The moorhen has very long toes. They help it to walk on soft mud and floating lily leaves.

The heron has long legs. They help it to walk through shallow water where it catches fish with its long beak.

The coot uses its beak to pull up underwater plants which it eats.

Heron

Moorhen

Coot

Dabchick

Pochard

Mallard drake

Mallard duck

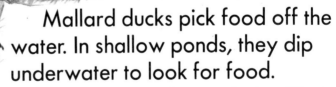

Mallard ducks pick food off the water. In shallow ponds, they dip underwater to look for food.

Pochard are diving ducks. The males, or drakes, are brightly coloured.

The little dabchick is good at diving and swimming underwater.

Insects and Amphibians

Like all other insects, water insects lay eggs. Larvae or nymphs hatch from the eggs. Later, these turn into adult insects.

Some larvae can eat things as big as themselves. On the right, you can see a larva of a great diving beetle eating a tadpole.

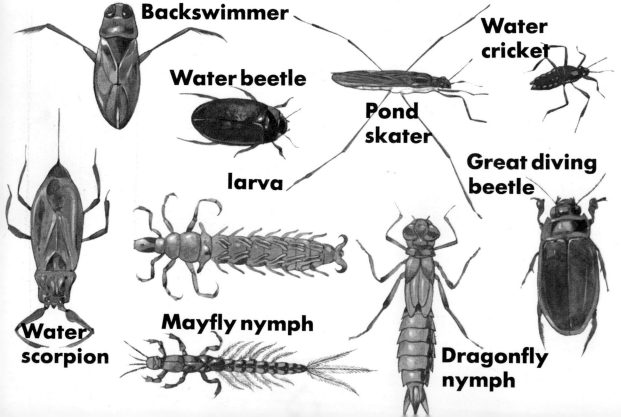

Beetle larva

Backswimmer

Water cricket

Water beetle

Pond skater

larva

Great diving beetle

Water scorpion

Mayfly nymph

Dragonfly nymph

Great diving beetle

Amphibians, like toads, frogs and newts, live on land and in water.

Toads have long tongues which they shoot out to catch flies.

Frogs sometimes change colour to match the things around them.

Male newts grow crests along their backs in the spring.

Newt

Frog

Toad

Fishes of the Pond

Fish lay eggs which hatch into tiny, new fish after a few days. Their bodies are protected by scales and by a slimy liquid which covers them. They use their tails to push themselves forward and their fins to steer.

Some fish, like rudd and roach, swim in groups called shoals.

Perch

Tench

Roach

Rudd

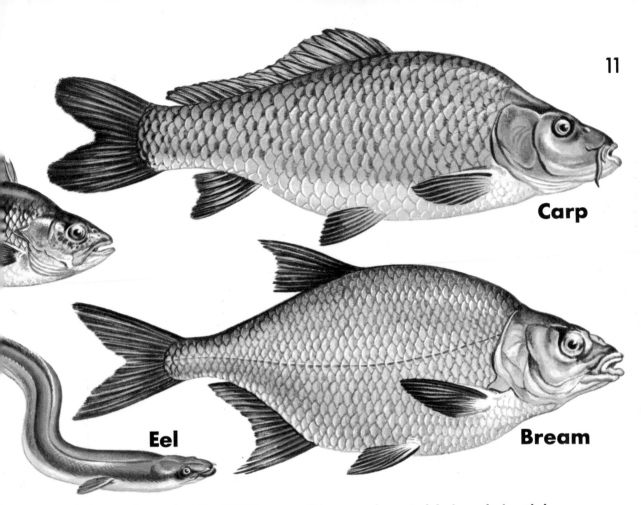

Carp

Eel

Bream

Sticklebacks guarding eggs

The male stickleback builds nests. His bright colour attracts the female. She lays her eggs inside his nest and swims away. The male stays to guard the eggs until they hatch. Then he looks after the young sticklebacks until they can look after themselves (left).

Many kinds of snail live in ponds.
The great pond snail scrapes food into its mouth with its rough tongue. It lays its eggs in strips called egg ropes (right).
The swan mussel lives in the mud. It opens its shells and puts out a foot. The foot holds on to the mud and pulls the mussel along.

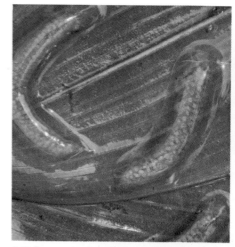

(Above) egg ropes

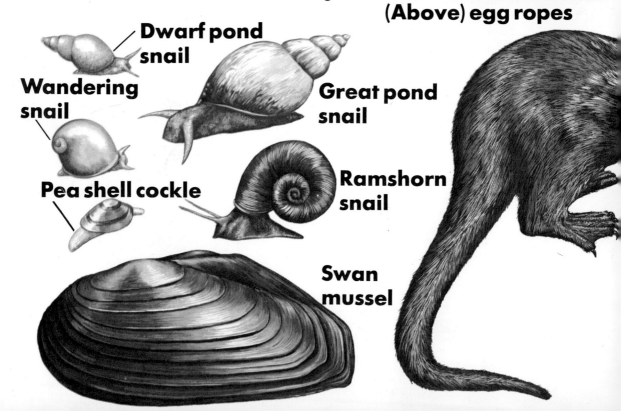

Dwarf pond snail

Wandering snail

Great pond snail

Pea shell cockle

Ramshorn snail

Swan mussel

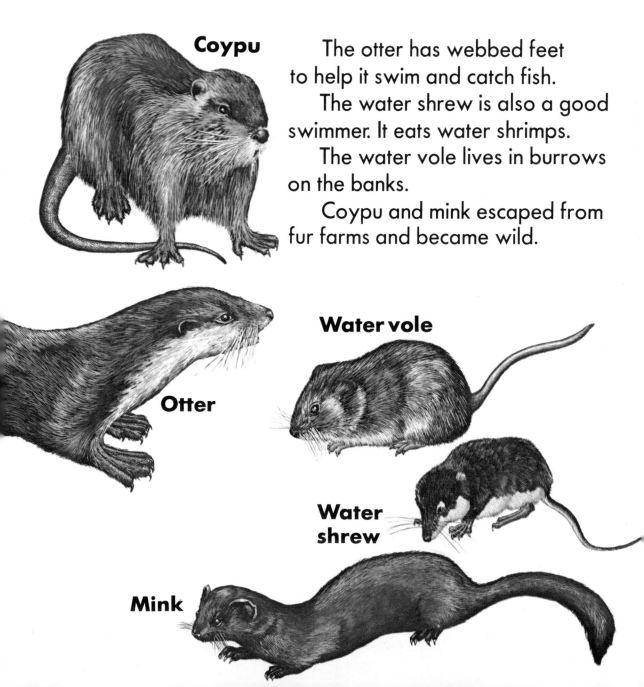

Coypu

The otter has webbed feet to help it swim and catch fish.

The water shrew is also a good swimmer. It eats water shrimps.

The water vole lives in burrows on the banks.

Coypu and mink escaped from fur farms and became wild.

Otter

Water vole

Water shrew

Mink

Stream Life

The water in streams is always moving. The kinds of animal and plant life you will find depends on the speed of the current.
This slow stream hardly disturbs wildlife at all (below).

The crack willow tree and sallow grow beside streams.
Water mint grows in the shallow water of streams. It has a pleasant scent.

Crack willow

Crayfish

Starwort

The dipper has to walk underwater to catch the insect larvae which it eats.

Caddis fly larvae and mayfly and stonefly nymphs turn into adult insects near the surface of the water. Brown trout eat them.

Mayfly

Caddis fly

Burr-reed

Forget-me-not

Stonefly

Sallow

Water mint

Dipper

Brown trout

Freshwater shrimp

Watercress

The tail of the pied wagtail bobs up and down as the bird paddles at the edge of the stream.

The kingfisher sits on a branch and dives for fish (right). It lays its eggs in a tunnel in the bank.

Pied wagtail

Dipper

Reed warbler

Grey wagtail

The grey wagtail makes its nest in cracks in the rock. It also makes its nest in the banks of streams, close to the running water.

The reed warbler makes a cup-shaped nest. It builds the nest by weaving grass through the stems of reeds.

Insects and Shell Life

When a dragonfly nymph is fully grown, it waits for a sunny day. Then it crawls out of the water and up a stem. Slowly its skin dries and splits. The adult dragonfly comes out (1). Its wings stretch in the sunshine (2). Then it flies away to catch other insects to eat.

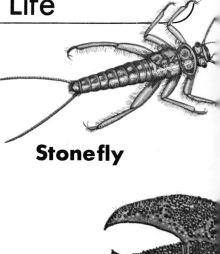

Stonefly

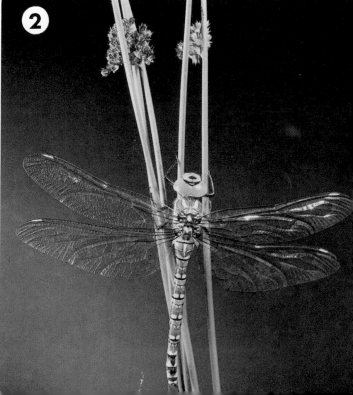

Crayfish

Caddis fly

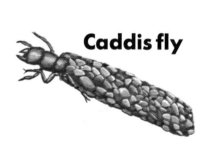

Freshwater shrimp

The crayfish walks along on eight legs. As it grows, its old skin comes off and leaves a new skin underneath. The new skin soon hardens to protect the crayfish.

The caddis fly larva lives in a case that it makes from leaves or from pebbles.

Dace

Bullhead

Pike

Lamprey

Barbel

Pike hide among the underwater plants and wait for smaller fish to swim by. Then they quickly grab the fish in their large jaws. Pike have many large, sharp teeth.

The bullhead, or miller's thumb, has sharp spines on its fins. These stop water birds and other fish attacking the bullhead.

The lamprey's mouth is like a sucker. It holds on to other fish with its mouth and feeds on them.

Barbel use the feelers hanging from their mouths to feel for worms and insects which they eat.

Young fish, like the trout on the right, are called fry.

(Above) trout fry

Minnow

Gudgeon

Glossary

Amphibians   Creatures which live on land as well as in the water.

Barbel   A kind of fish which has feelers hanging from its mouth. The feelers themselves are also called barbels.

Burrow   A hole dug by an animal in which it lives and takes shelter.

Current   Water flowing in one direction.

Drake   A male duck.

Duck   A kind of water bird. Duck is also the name for the female bird of this kind.

Egg rope   A band of eggs laid by creatures such as the great pond snail.

Fin   Part of a fish. Fins stick out from the sides of fishes' bodies. The fish use their fins to steer themselves through the water.

Fry   Young fish.

Larva   A creature which hatches from an insect's egg but does not look like its parents.

Nymph   A creature which hatches from an insect's egg and looks like its parents.

Scales   Thin, tough, overlapping plates which cover the bodies of fish and protect the skin underneath.

Shoal   A group of fish swimming together.

Index

Barbel   21
Brown trout   15
Caddis fly   4, 15, 19
Coot   6
Coypu   13
Crack willow   14
Crayfish   14, 19
Dabchick   7
Dipper   15, 16
Dragonfly   18
Fish   6, 10, 13, 20, 21
Frog   5, 9
Fry   2
Great pond snail   12
Heron   6
Kingfisher   5, 16
Mallard   7
Mayfly   15
Mink   13
Moorhen   6
Newt   4, 5, 9

Otter   13
Pochard   7
Pond mussel   12
Reeds   4, 5
Reed warbler   17
Sallow   14, 15
Shrimp   13, 15, 19
Snail   12
Stickleback   11
Stonefly   15, 18
Toad   5, 9
Wagtail   16, 17
Water beetle   8
Water boatman   4
Water lily   4, 5
Water mint   14, 15
Water scorpion   5, 8
Water shrew   12, 13
Water spider   4
Water vole   5, 13
Whirligig beetle   4

Photo credits: Heather Angel, MSc, FRPS, Natural History Photographic Agency, Natural Science Photos, Oxford Scientific Films Ltd., John Topham Picture Library

1 2 3 4 5 6 7 8 9 10— R —85 84 83 82 81